Fact Finders®

Theme Park Science

ENERGY at the THEME PARK

by Karen Latchana Kenney

raintree
a Capstone company — publishers for children

Raintree is an imprint of Capstone Global Library Limited, a company incorporated in England and Wales having its registered office at 264 Banbury Road, Oxford, OX2 7DY – Registered company number: 6695582

www.raintree.co.uk
myorders@raintree.co.uk

Text © Capstone Global Library Limited 2020
The moral rights of the proprietor have been asserted.

All rights reserved. No part of this publication may be reproduced in any form or by any means (including photocopying or storing it in any medium by electronic means and whether or not transiently or incidentally to some other use of this publication) without the written permission of the copyright owner, except in accordance with the provisions of the Copyright, Designs and Patents Act 1988 or under the terms of a licence issued by the Copyright Licensing Agency, Barnard's Inn, 86 Fetter Lane, London, EC4A 1EN (www.cla.co.uk). Applications for the copyright owner's written permission should be addressed to the publisher.

Edited by Carrie Braulick Sheely
Designed by Tracy McCabe
Original illustrations © Capstone Global Library Limited 2020
Picture research by Eric Gohl
Production by Kathy McColley
Originated by Capstone Global Library Ltd
Printed and bound in India

978 1 4747 8511 2 (hardback)
978 1 4747 8515 0 (paperback)

British Library Cataloguing in Publication Data
A full catalogue record for this book is available from the British Library.

Acknowledgements
We would like to thank the following for permission to reproduce photographs: Alamy: Bill Brooks, 17 (bottom), James Nesterwitz, 11, Serge Bogomyako, 13 (top), 25; iStockphoto: CasarsaGuru, 15, Nikada, back cover (background), 23 (top); Newscom: Image Source/Jon Feingersh Photography Inc., 13 (bottom), Splash News/Duke Energy, 23 (bottom); Shutterstock: Chad Verzosa, 21, Claudio Zaccherini, 9, corbac40, 19 (bottom), KateChris, 20, Krylovochka, cover (bottom), 1 (bottom), Matsuo Sato, 29, Paper Cat, 5, Racheal Grazias, 1 (background), 7, 19 (top), SAHACHATZ, 17 (top), Standret, 27, Titima Ongkantong, 24, Yicai, cover (top). Design elements: Shutterstock.

Every effort has been made to contact copyright holders of material reproduced in this book. Any omissions will be rectified in subsequent printings if notice is given to the publisher.

All the internet addresses (URLs) given in this book were valid at the time of going to press. However, due to the dynamic nature of the internet, some addresses may have changed, or sites may have changed or ceased to exist since publication. While the author and publisher regret any inconvenience this may cause readers, no responsibility for any such changes can be accepted by either the author or the publisher.

CONTENTS

Chapter 1
Energy all around! 4

Chapter 2
Potential and kinetic energy 6

Chapter 3
The buzz on electricity 12

Chapter 4
Hot snacks, cold treats
and lots of heat 18

Chapter 5
Bright lights and loud sounds 24

Chapter 6
An exploding end to the fun 28

Glossary 30
Comprehension questions 31
Find out more 31
Index 32

CHAPTER 1
ENERGY ALL AROUND!

Put on some comfy shoes and get ready! You're about to enter a theme park! You'll fly through the air on your favourite rides, scream as loud as you can and eat some delicious treats. It will be a great day! But have you ever wondered what makes all this fun possible? Energy works behind the scenes all around a theme park.

Energy is the power to do work. People use energy in different ways. Energy cannot be created or destroyed. But energy can be changed, or transformed.

How is energy at work in a theme park? Energy can become motion for rides that spin, flip and dive. Energy can become heat you can feel, light you can see and sound you can hear.

What are you waiting for? Let's see how energy is involved in all the park's hair-raising thrills!

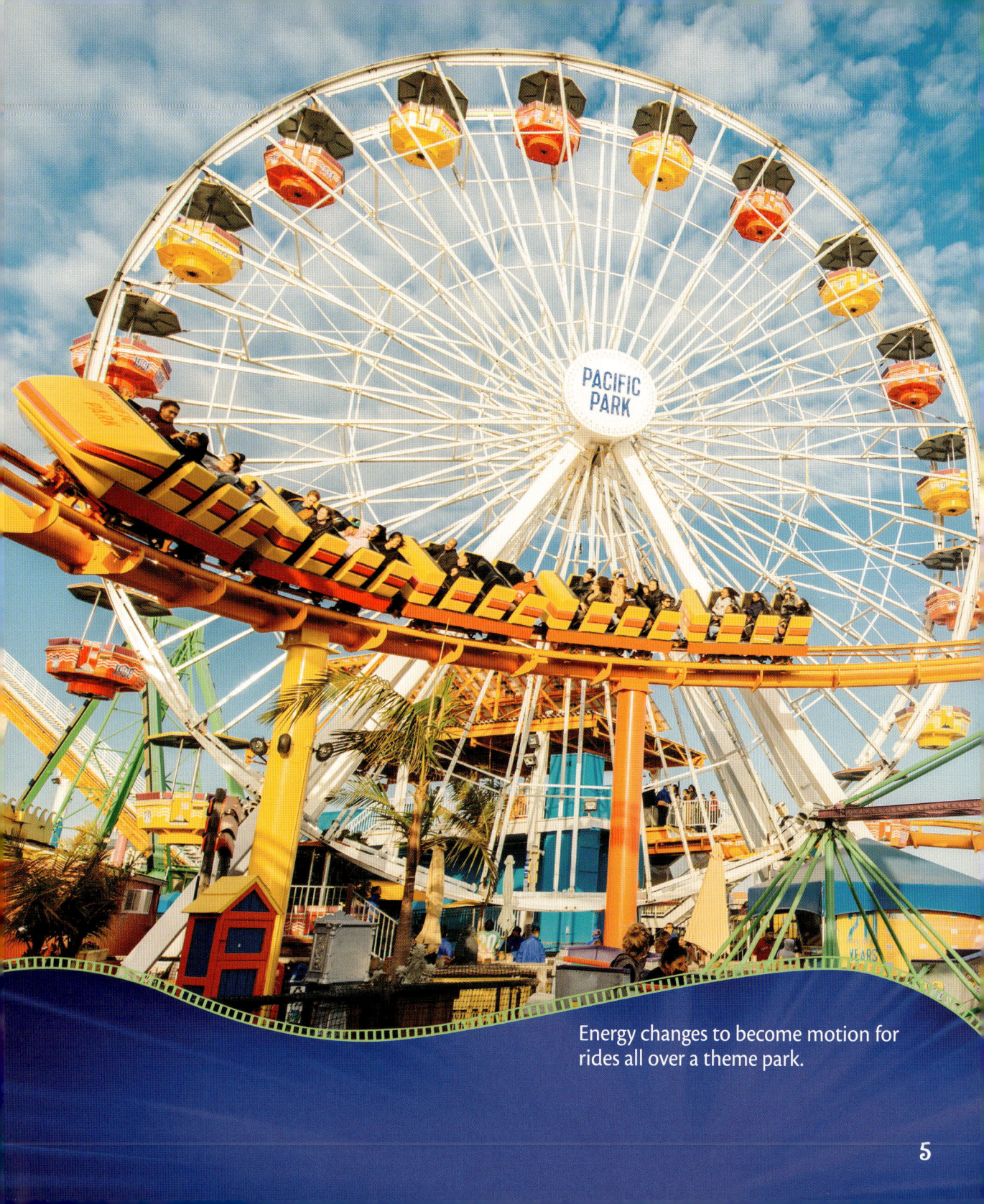

Energy changes to become motion for rides all over a theme park.

CHAPTER 2
POTENTIAL AND KINETIC ENERGY

Click, click, click. You're on the biggest, wildest roller coaster at the park. The cars crawl up the first hill. It's high – really high! That clicking sound comes from a machine. It pulls the cars up the hill with a cable.

The hill is high for a reason. As the cars climb higher, they gain more **potential energy**. The cars will use this stored energy to zoom around the track.

As soon as the cars go over the hill, the potential energy changes to **kinetic energy**. Gravity pulls the cars down the hill. This force attracts all objects towards the centre of Earth. *"Aaaahhhh!"* Riders scream and laugh as they free fall. The cars rush up and down the track. They zip around twists and turns. The hills get smaller and smaller. The cars have less and less kinetic energy to move. Soon the ride slows to a stop.

> **kinetic energy** energy of a moving object
> **potential energy** energy stored within an object, waiting to be released

As soon as a roller coaster goes over the first hill, its energy changes to kinetic energy.

FACT
When you're in free fall, you experience weightlessness. Your stomach feels strange. Scientists think the fast downward rush makes some of your organs move a bit. They float up as you fall down.

Pendulum power

Now for the **pendulum** ride, and it's a real rush. The part of the ride you sit in is attached to a long arm. The arm slowly starts swinging from one side to the other. You go higher and higher. Then you loop all the way around before speeding back down.

What's behind this excitement? Pendulum rides build up potential energy as they rise. Then gravity pulls the ride down. Just like on a roller coaster, the potential energy changes to kinetic energy. The ride swings at its **axis** from side to side. Its energy swaps back and forth from potential to kinetic as it rises higher and falls back down. When the ride is at its highest, it has the most potential energy. When it is moving fastest, it has the most kinetic energy. This kinetic energy powers the ride into a full loop.

axis real or imaginary line through the centre of an object, around which the object turns

pendulum weight that hangs from a fixed point and swings back and forth freely using the force of gravity

A pendulum ride has the most potential energy when it reaches the highest point.

FACT
Pendulums can be used to keep time in clocks. Dutch scientist Christiaan Huygens invented the first pendulum clock in 1656.

Catapult up!

If you think the pendulum ride didn't get you high enough into the sky, try the catapult ride! The seats are connected to two cables. The cables go to the top of two tall towers and over **pulleys**. The cables go back down to the ground inside the towers. The other ends of the cables attach to stretchy springs inside a small spring tower near the two taller towers. When the seats are released, you rocket up. You fly past the tops of the towers. You're so high up that people on the ground look like ants!

Hundreds of stretchy springs fling this ride upwards. Inside the spring tower, a metal plate is at the top and bottom of the springs. A **hydraulic** system pulls the plates apart. This stretches the springs, giving them potential energy called elastic energy. When the seats are released, the potential energy in the springs becomes kinetic energy. The bottom plate flies up in the spring tower. This pulls on the cables. It makes the seats fly up into the air. The springs and seats bounce up and down. Finally they slow down, and it's time to get off. Phew! You made it!

When potential energy changes to kinetic energy, the catapult ride's seat launches high into the air.

hydraulic having to do with a system powered by fluid forced through pipes or chambers

pulley grooved wheel turned by a rope, belt or chain

FACT
Some catapult rides get the seats more than 100 metres (350 feet) in the air.

CHAPTER 3
THE BUZZ ON ELECTRICITY

Strap yourself in and get ready to drive! We're going on the bumper cars next. The cars move in every direction. You stomp on the pedal. *Bump!* You crash into another car. You reverse and you're on to the next car. But how do they run?

Bumper car tracks are wired for **electrical energy** (electricity). Electrical energy comes from **atoms**. Atoms are tiny particles. Everything is made from atoms. Each atom has a positive and negative electric charge. At the centre of an atom is a nucleus. Electrons spin around the nucleus. Usually the electrons stay close to their atoms. But sometimes they move and leave their atoms. When electrons are free to flow from atom to atom, they create electricity.

> **atom** element in its smallest form
>
> **electrical energy** energy that results from the flow of charged particles, such as electrons, or from a build-up of charged particles on an object

Electricity powers bumper cars as well as many other rides at a theme park.

AN ELECTRIC DISCOVERY

The ancient Greeks are said to have discovered electricity about 2,500 years ago. But this was a different type of electricity than the one we use today to power machines. The type of electricity the Greeks discovered is called static electricity. It results from a material having too many or too few electrons. An electrical charge builds up on an object. This is the same type of energy that makes your hair stand on end after you rub a balloon against it. The rubbing removes electrons from the balloon and adds them to your hair. The hair's negative charge is attracted to the balloon's positive charge.

Today, people make electricity in different ways. One of the ways we make electricity is at a power station. The power station sends electricity through wires to other places, such as theme parks. Once there, the electricity can be used to power rides such as the bumper cars.

There are different bumper car systems, but they all use electricity. Some types of bumper cars have long metal poles. The poles connect to a grid on the top of the track. Parts under the vehicle connect to the floor. Electricity flows through the grid and the floor. The cars connect to both positive and negative charges through the floor and grid. This completes an electrical circuit. A circuit is a path that electrons can flow through. Electricity flows into the cars and powers their motors. Then a wheel under the car rolls. The electricity is now kinetic energy, and the cars move.

FACT
The first bumper cars in the early 1920s were sometimes called dodgems. They were not made to bump into one another. Instead, drivers tried to avoid (dodge) crashes.

Bumper cars often have poles attached to them that connect to a ceiling grid.

Electricity behind the scenes

Rides get all the attention at a theme park, but they wouldn't work without control systems. Control systems make the rides move and keep them safe. They control which parts of rides get power. Engineers design computers specifically for a park's control systems. Computer programmers make **software** for the systems. These systems all need electricity to run.

software programs that tell the hardware of a computer what to do

Because the control systems are so important, a park has generators if the electricity is ever cut off from the power station. A generator is a machine that can create electricity. It uses fuel to move a magnet around a coil of wires. This movement makes a flow of electrons. The generator's electricity can then be used.

A storm's rolling in!

Electricity can be in the air at a park too. Can you see that storm cloud rolling in? In the distance, lightning strikes. Did you know that you've just seen electricity? In the storm cloud, bits of ice bump into one another as they move around. These collisions (bumps) build up an electrical charge. The top part of the cloud has a positive charge and the bottom part has a negative charge. When the positive and negative charges become big enough, a giant spark occurs between the two charges in the cloud. We call this big spark lightning. The spark can also occur between a cloud and the ground.

Lightning that reaches the ground is called cloud-to-ground lightning.

POWERING DISNEY WORLD

Disney World is a big theme park in Florida, USA. It covers about 104 square kilometres (40 square miles). That's almost the same size as the city of Liverpool! The park uses so much electricity that it has its own power station. The station provides some of the park's power through an underground system.

CHAPTER 4

HOT SNACKS, COLD TREATS AND LOTS OF HEAT

The storm is going to miss us after all. You've been on some rides and waited in long queues. Now the sun is high in the sky. Sunlight changes to heat. The air temperature rises. You're starting to sweat and get a bit tired. The fun's not over yet, but you need a break! Time for some snacks and treats. You can see how energy cooks and cools food.

Heat is made from moving atoms. These atoms are in all **matter**. As an object's atoms move faster, its temperature gets hotter. As heat is taken away, the object's atoms move more slowly. Its temperature drops. Heat naturally moves from hotter objects to cooler objects. This heat transfer makes objects change temperature.

matter anything that has weight and takes up space

On a clear day the sun heats up everything at a theme park.

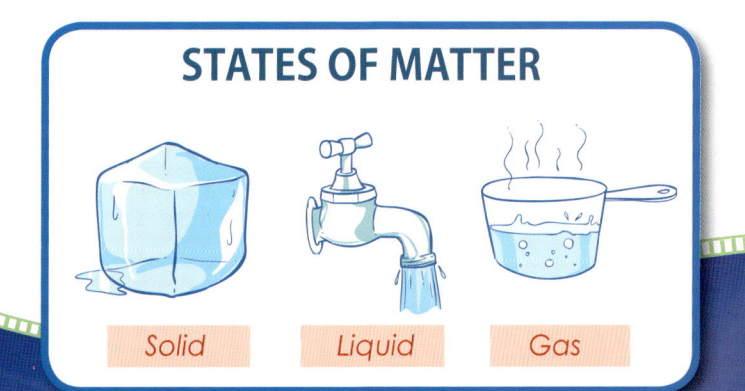

STATES OF MATTER

Solid　　Liquid　　Gas

FACT
The type of matter affects how atoms move. In solids they move slowly. In liquid they move faster. In gases atoms move even faster.

At the park, heat makes the treats you love to eat. Can't wait to bite into that fluffy candyfloss? This super-sweet treat comes from grains of sugar. Heat turns the grains into long threads. A candyfloss machine uses electricity to heat up the grains of sugar. The sugar's atoms move faster and faster. Soon the sugar turns into liquid. At the same time, the machine spins. The liquid sugar shoots out through small holes in the metal container around it. The liquid quickly cools as it shoots out, making tiny threads of sugar. Then the threads are wrapped onto a stick, and it's ready to eat!

Sugar heats up to form candyfloss.

Snow cone zone

Maybe you're in the mood for a snow cone. Did you know that even cold things have heat? Snow cones are made of shaved ice. This ice was once liquid water. When water goes into a freezer, its temperature drops to below 0 degrees Celsius (32 degrees Fahrenheit). Heat flows from the water into the air. The water's atoms slow down. They almost stop moving. The water changes from liquid into the solid we know as ice. The ice is shaved into a cone and some fruity syrup is added. Now you can take a bite!

FACT
Dentist William Morrison and sweet maker John C. Wharton created candyfloss in 1897.

You'd better eat your snow cone fast, though! Before long, it will melt. Everything's getting hot in the sun, from the pavement to the metal bars on the rides. Energy from the Sun travels through the air as light. We call the Sun's energy **solar energy**. When the light hits Earth, it transforms into heat as it hits different materials, such as the ground, air, water and pavement. It heats up your snow cone too. Atoms move faster inside the ice of your snow cone and it melts. As you finish the rest of your snow cone, your body sweats to help you keep cool. The sweat **evaporates** into the air. It takes some body heat away with it.

---

evaporate change from a liquid to a gas
solar energy energy from the Sun

From the pavement to rides, solar energy causes objects at a theme park to become hotter.

SOLAR-POWERED PARKS

Solar energy can do much more than heat up a theme park. It can also help to power a park. Solar panels gather sunlight and turn it into electricity. The process of using solar panels to make electricity is better for the environment than other ways of producing electricity. Legoland in Florida, USA, uses solar energy to power part of its park. In 2018, Disney began building a new 109-hectare (270-acre) solar facility in central Florida. They also announced plans for a similar facility at Disneyland Paris, which would provide 15 per cent of the park's electricity.

Disney's current solar park is in the shape of Mickey Mouse.

CHAPTER 5

BRIGHT LIGHTS AND LOUD SOUNDS

Shouts and laughter roar from the roller coaster. The cars make a loud *whoosh* as they pass by. Lively music cranks out from the merry-go-round. Sounds are everywhere at the park. They travel through the air. Some sounds are loud and some are quiet. Some sounds have a low pitch; others have a high pitch. What makes these sounds?

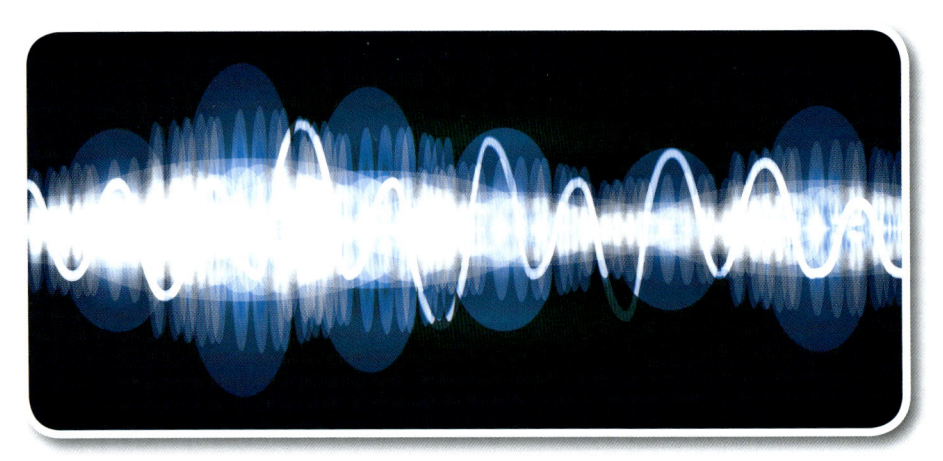

Sound travels through the air in waves.

When an object vibrates, it moves matter. The energy in the vibrating movement transfers into the air. It moves in waves. These **sound waves** move one after the other until they reach your ears. They make your eardrums vibrate. The tiny hairs inside your ears pick up the sounds. They turn them into signals for your brain. That's how you hear all the sounds of the park. The loudness or quietness of a sound depends on the sound wave's strength, or **amplitude**. The pitch of a sound depends on the speed of the waves. If the sound waves move slowly, you hear a low-pitched sound. If they are fast, you hear a high-pitched sound.

amplitude distance from the mid-point of a wave to its crest; a measure of wave strength

sound wave wave or vibration that can be heard

As roller coaster riders scream, sound waves travel through the air.

Lighting up the night

As night-time nears, the park lights up. The rides twinkle with bright lights. Colourful lights shine on stages as shows begin. Energy from electricity changes into light we can see.

Light comes from a source, such as a light bulb on a ride or the Sun. It's made of tiny parts called photons. This energy moves in waves from its source. It moves in all directions as it spreads out. Light is very bright at its source. It gets dimmer and dimmer the further it goes.

When light waves reach our eyes, they enter our eye lens. The waves move to the back of our eyes and hit rods and cones. The rods and cones send messages to our brain so that we can see.

Lights from rides shine brightly at night.

FACT
Lasers are a special type of light. They have waves that line up very closely. This makes the light very bright. The waves create a thin beam of light that travels far without losing much energy.

27

CHAPTER 6

AN EXPLODING END TO THE FUN

Boom! Suddenly lights explode high above you. Red, green and blue streak across the night sky. A burning smell drifts through the air. It's the end of the night, and this is the fireworks display you've been waiting for all day.

These fireworks are the result of energy stored inside chemicals. Energy is released during a chemical reaction. With fireworks, fire makes that reaction happen. It burns gunpowder. Other chemicals and explosive materials are also inside the fireworks. As they burn, the materials release heat and gas. The heat and gas trigger chemical reactions. The released gas creates a big boom. Mixtures of different metals and salts inside the fireworks determine what colour the lights will be as they burn.

Chemical reactions are behind the amazing fireworks displays at theme parks.

It's been an exciting day at the theme park. Energy was everywhere. It moved from place to place and changed again and again. From wild rides to tasty treats and loud screams, energy keeps theme parks filled with thrills.

GLOSSARY

amplitude distance from the mid-point of a wave to its crest; a measure of wave strength

atom element in its smallest form

axis real or imaginary line through the centre of an object, around which the object turns

electrical energy energy that results from the flow of charged particles, such as electrons, or from a build-up of charged particles on an object

evaporate change from a liquid to a gas

hydraulic having to do with a system powered by fluid forced through pipes or chambers

kinetic energy energy of a moving object

matter anything that has weight and takes up space

pendulum weight that hangs from a fixed point and swings back and forth freely using the force of gravity

potential energy energy stored within an object, waiting to be released

pulley grooved wheel turned by a rope, belt or chain

software programs that tell the hardware of a computer what to do

solar energy energy from the Sun

sound wave vibration that can be heard

Comprehension Questions

1. What is the difference between potential and kinetic energy?

2. Read pages 6–9. What type of energy does electricity change to once it powers a motor to make a machine move?

3. Sound moves in waves from a source. Why do you think sounds are quieter the further you are from their source? Why are they louder when you are closer to the source?

Find Out More

Books

Energy (DK Eyewitness), Dan Green (DK Children, 2016)

Energy (DKfindout!), Emily Dodd (DK Children, 2018)

From Falling Water to Electric Car: An energy journey through the world of electricity (Energy Journeys), Ian Graham (Raintree, 2016)

Solar Energy (Energy Revolution), Karen Latchana Kenney (Raintree, 2019)

Websites

www.bbc.co.uk/bitesize/articles/zsgwwxs
Learn more about the states of matter.

www.dkfindout.com/uk/science/energy/types-energy
Find out more about different types of energy.

INDEX

amplitude 25
ancient Greeks 13
atoms 12, 18, 19, 20, 22
axis 8

bumper cars 12, 14

candyfloss 20
catapult ride 10
computer programmers 15
control systems 15

Disneyland Paris 23
Disney World 17, 23

electricity 12, 13, 14, 15, 16, 17, 20, 23, 26
electrons 12, 13, 14, 16
engineers 15
evaporation 22

fireworks 28
free fall 6, 7

heat 4, 18, 20, 23, 28
hydraulics 10

kinetic energy 6, 8, 10, 14

lasers 27
light 4, 22, 26, 27, 28
lightning 16

matter 18, 19, 25
motion 4

nucleus 12

pendulum 8, 10
photons 26
potential energy 6, 8, 10
power stations 14, 16, 17
pulleys 10

roller coasters 6, 8, 24

snow cones 21
software 15
solar energy 22, 23
sound waves 25
static electricity 13
sunlight 18, 23